DATE DUF

Spirits Distilled

Spirits Distilled

Poems

: :

JEFFREY LAMAR COLEMAN

RED HEN PRESS | Los Angeles, California

SPIRITS DISTILLED

Cover image: *Spirits Distilled 2005*,
mixed media collage, 13" x 15".
Copyright 2005 © Wendell George Brown.
Used by permission.

Book and cover design by Mark E. Cull

ISBN: 1-59709-049-2
Library of Congress Catalog Card Number: 2005927958

Published by Red Hen Press

The City of Los Angeles Cultural Affairs Department, California Arts Council, Los Angeles County Arts Commission and National Endowment for the Arts partially support Red Hen Press.

First Edition

Acknowledgements

The author gratefully acknowledges the editors of the following publications in which some of the poems herein first appeared, sometimes in slightly different form:

Brilliant Corners: A Journal of Jazz and Literature: "Blues Sarcoma"; *Sycamore Review*: "Rivers Between Us—for Gwendolyn Brooks"; "Milosevic's Evening Soliloquy"; *Journal of Social and Political Thought*: "Regions"; "Words, Sweet and Absolute"; "Body Art Theatre"; "Separation"; *RATTLE: Poetry for the 21st Century*: "The Season for Fathers"; *Blue Mesa Review*: "Onslaught in the Upper Western Hemisphere"; "Alone in Presence of Air"; *Black Bear Review*: "The Isolated Road—for James Byrd, Jr."; *Weavings 2000: The Maryland Millennial Anthology*: "Morning Quatrains—for Ynez."

CONTENTS

IV :: *Incantations*

V :: *Hunger's Embrace*

Jeffrey Lamar Coleman explores in this volume the power of silence, in a world filled with words. The poems wrestle with language and meaning, with truth and myth, at times finding the tongue can be fleshless, the words useless. There is hope however, our world though "often lonely" does not leave us alone. This is a fine and brave collection and it introduces a young poet of grace and understanding.

—Lucille Clifton

I :: *Spirits Distilled*

I will have the gardeners come to me and recite
Many flowers, and in the small clay pots
Of their melodious names I will bring back
Some remnant of the hundred fragrances.

—Rilke

The Isolated Road

for James Byrd, Jr.

Does it always dissect night veins
With a precision that flows
Fluid as blood coursing through
Endless oval chains, iron
In the shape of a surprised man's mouth
No longer able to gasp—
Or does it sometimes ripen and age,
Feral, like lost ancestry, waiting
For the right moon to strike
Flesh and joints, or
Newsprint against early morning doors:
The torn and battered body
Of James Byrd Jr., 49, was discovered
Sunday morning in a wooded area . . .
The head and right arm were missing.
The body parts, apparently severed
As Byrd was dragged
Along a two-mile stretch of the isolated road,
Were found a mile away . . .

Broken into poetry that confounds
Every human metaphor,
We are entwined like ghosts
Unable to escape the other's home.
How should I tell my children

I am murdered nightly in my dreams,
Or once, as a child, I rejoiced
When a chicken was yanked,
Its body circling the farm till dusk
While its white feathery head throbbed
Like fear in my grandfather's palm?

Rivers Between Us

for Gwendolyn Brooks

". . . almost secretly, I had always felt that to be black was good."
She intended this as entendre, layered
As mythology you and I should find
Authentic, fictitious, something along the lines of writing
The complexity of whiteness,
How it's empty, omnipotent, and always there
Rushing to cover its nakedness.
I saw it again last weekend

At Harper's Ferry when a young man stood and shouted,
"John Brown was a goddamn traitor!"
His voice as convinced as wounded Gray,
His fingers webbed shut against his palms,
And his eyes staring for the first time
Into a photograph never taken, a landscape still detonating
Up through his gut after one hundred and forty years.
He takes a handkerchief from his right rear pocket

And sweat disappears, dissolving into thirteen folded stars
Stuffed neatly back inside faded denim. "Wish he was still around,
I'd hang him my damn self," he says, and from top of the Blue Ridge
With sun singing down, I could have sworn I saw five hazy ghosts
The color of a thousand carved muskets—but I was wrong
It was a blur of Confederate soldiers
Descending in blackface, cakewalking, and yelling something
As I stood there staring

At the sight of it all—straddling centuries like wreckage,
One foot in the Potomac and the other the Shenandoah.
That's when her words circled back
Up through those waters, and again I felt some sense
Of voices, what they must have been like
When first she donned that haunting laurel—
Jagged curses of whispers rising
From all corners and hallowed streets.

Driving home with the scene behind me, I kept hearing
Somehow to find a still spot in the noise
Was the frayed inner want, the winding, the frayed hope
And once more I knew what I had known for years:
Allegiance flows twice, at times, or not at all,
As if the compass once carried can no longer be read.
Utterances of smoke still detected in the distance, but you're not sure
How they got there, who's leading the charge, fanning the flames.

Milosevic's Evening Soliloquy

How much longer
Can I allow it to devour
Everything I no longer am? The world

Why do we think it wants us
Destroyed, or destroying? A stone
I once cast through the galaxy

Struck an unsuspecting star. The star
Landed and burned an entire village.
I am told, no survivors, that I was young,

Not yet who I am.
I pleaded, "It was an accident!"
One clear and imperfect evening.

Now a raft of words and bones
Floats beyond the distance
Beneath me.

I have sacrificed them all:
Every unclothed syllable
Now stares back.

I am motionless, speechless
Without them. I have become silent
In their absence: nothing now

But the roar of homes torched,
Collapsing from north to south
Across ashes of earth,

The dust of all that remains
Buried—remnants, images
And names still smoldering.

Missteps and calculations, yes,
Gone wrong, as if hairs of wire
Too soon tripped, or mines

Again rupturing clouds over mountains.
Down comes a stream
Of forgotten flesh, and I gaze

Into this crown, lined and jeweled
With chaos. Once more,
I steady myself

One foot sinking, and imagine leaping,
Arms outstretched, like a winged savior
Neither penitent nor yet crucified

But no longer hailed, staring
Into darkened sky, and shaking
Fists of bones at gods.

Slobodan's Predawn Letter to Mirjana

No new moons for months now
And nothing flows but noise of you

Battering silent air sheets in the distance.
And if I were to throw my screams

A thousand times inside a broken breeze
I still would not reach you. Once,

I thought I had: Your mouth opened,
And a stream of words

Came in familiar rhythms,
But disappeared

Before I could write them.
I have tried to recapture so much of you—

The flesh we once felt
The sound of hungry birds

Pecking at the window feeder, but
In this state of captured days,

Only fragments in which your words scattered
Remain. It's not so much I need to gather

Or unite them, as that they now reside
In so many corridors of thought.

The doors, when opened,
Reveal much more than an image

Of countless rats trapped.
And, when I'm restless

Dazed from their ramblings,
They escape to topple the crown:

They come always at this hour
For they know I cannot defend my back

Glued by their legs to my bed
I cannot move

As they claw closer with breath
Feeding teeth to my ears

And eating all the silence
I need to forget.

Virtual Memories of a Prehuman Subject

for Sally Hemmings

It is the infinite possibility, not the finite
That drives us, alone for years and days
While two oblique swans drown
Down near the bottom
Of old man Jefferson's lake.

There was a fire there one evening
And Sally's children danced along the shore
With a sense of graceful confusion
Only young slaves can achieve.

I turned to see if she was watching,
But she had walked away
To sit beneath a sky of trees.
After all, it was Spring
And rain was saying hello
To everything in its path.

Did she happen to glance the clouds
When words fell from his tongue,
When lightning struck
Her quarters in the far south distance,
Leaving only shadows where bodies once stood?

Please, do not tell me you do not understand.
We were all lovers once,
Both fictitious and sublime
Long before we discovered
The structure of genetic fear,
The fear of genetic structure.
Do you remember

Paintings on the ceilings of caves,
Or the way ambitious young birds
Evolved into dinosaurs and back again
With and without wings?
They, too, have left us
With slivers of bone under microscopes,

Listening to the wisdom
Of fossilized dung—tracing footprints
Of masters we never knew.

Their tracks are infinite
And dutiful in their memories
Of things not returning—
Or should I say things
It seems we are forever returning to?

Drifting Through Cemeteries

for James Baldwin

Snow: a ripple of satin
Swam from the sun

In rectangular shadows
To the place he stood

Covered in black and wind,
His eyes roaming the field

Of chiseled markers.
They fell. Words

Like snowflakes kissed
Goodbye, or crescents

Fractured along waves
Caressing the flow

Of evening. Rows of earth
Behind him disappeared: spaces

He entered, leaving
Like newborn ink

Sings across a fresh white sheet.

Choosing My Father's Coffin

The scent of mountain laurel fading in late spring
Overlooking St. Mary's River,
An orchestra of insects guiding sand, pebble, and notions
Of the sacred home again. I think of my mother,
How she has always lived inland
Close to her own mother's music,
How, if I breathe silently enough, I can almost hear
Chords of "Dixie" and "Amazing Grace"
Synchronized to damn and release
One's heart to an open field.

There, she kneels whispering
With eyes drawn to grass and earth.
Two, three, or four times a week
Her hushed offerings find their way
Through red mounded dirt
Layered with plastic wreaths
That smell like Foster's Funeral Home.

We selected the color, size, and price
Of his coffin. Would his navy suit complement
The casket's lighter shade of blue?
Would his necktie pick up the red in his folded army flag?
The clock down the hall
From the undertaker's office seemed to tick
Each second louder than the next,
A steady mechanical drop of water
Hammering through our chests
Like an ancient form of pre-burial torture.

The Season for Fathers

I

Days before my thirty-fourth year
And a week prior to the bombings
You wrapped your arms around
Gabriel's ethereal horn
                         and left
The part of you we had always known
Stretched across the floor
Of Oxford Industries.
Motionless. A slight concrete gash
Above your right eye.

There had been nothing
In Monday's morning
That said, *gather*, or *soon*
Or *prepare*.
There had been no flags waving
On the backs of cool noon breezes.

When your co-worker found you, she screamed.
When her screams found me, I sank
Into childhood silence,
Watching a single blackbird
Touch down in a wave
Of yellow wildflowers.

I should have photographed the stillness.
I should have captured everything
Alive in the foreground of pre-spring sky.

II

I sat there staring at you, Dad,
Before Rufus, your ol' bowling pal
From the mortuary, lowered the lid.
You in your favorite navy blue suit
Reminding me of the rented tux
You wore by my side in Albuquerque.
                              Two years ago
You were my best man.
Now, in two weeks, we'll enter the season
For fathers.

Should I send flowers,
Sing your favorite spiritual,
Pray your favorite prayer?

What, Dad, in the presence
Of newfound absence,
Should a good son do?

Grandmother's Quilt

The year the Titanic sank
My grandmother was born.
She wasn't aboard
But the purple, orange, and yellow quilt
Her parents wrapped her in was majestic.
There were swirls, strokes, and dots
Drawn together by the piecework of their home—
Old blouses, skirts, and cloths.

The year she died
I promised I would write a poem for her.
They named her Altherea,
Which to my mind meant goddess,
Or the woman nothing earthly could ever sink.

II :: *The Long Woman Quartet*

It was way back there—the old folks told it—that Raw-Head-And-Bloody-Bones had reached down and laid hold of the taproot that points to the center of the world. . . . But they talked in people's language and nobody knew them but the old folks. . . . Nobody can say where it begins or ends. Mouths don't empty themselves unless the ears are sympathetic and knowing.

—Zora Neale Hurston

The Long Woman of Evening

The goat burns into his sleep,
Right side of body splayed
Across a nomad's gurney
Mouth half-open, as if to say,
Now, please. Hurry and be done.

Overhead, the twined bulb swings
Shadows under candles,
Against floor, wall, and blade.

They say she is a long woman
From a long line of long women,
The kind that can stretch your days
Into a million twisted nights,
Or bring you back across
From some dark and hungry place.

When she catches him by the neck
She rubs the leaves her fingers grow
Into his six-inch slit of evening.
Then a rolling rhythm sounds
Like, "Boogala, boogala"
As it dances from her gut.
Over and over and over
She presses palm into his throat.

Something in his body moves.

Her bare right foot steps back,
Toes sinking into the earth.

Again, something in his body moves.

She raises her hand,
Wraps arms around breasts
And shouts a three-tongued sermon
Loud enough to wake ancestral flowing dreams.

Somewhere a wild goat rises and runs
Crazy as the glories of Hell
Riding naked and bloodied
Through an aching man's head.

Visitations

Can you help me?
Please, can you help me?
He arrives, right arm carrying left waist,
Doubled-over and sweating.
His words unfurl in rasps of moans—
So hollow a hoot-owl turns
And courts three-quarter moon,
So lonesome a firefly flashes
Against star-dark sky.

Can you help me, he says,
Recalling around an open flame
His past three days:
How a concrete wall lured his eighteen-wheeler
How some thick green odor has become his piss
How, yesterday, the teeth of a distant mouth
Gnawed colon, muscle, gut.
Can you help me?

Long Woman sways before the fire,
Says nothing, stares a starer's stare,
The kind used one evening
To drive six dogs against each other—
Only one muzzle gleaming
Once the snarls of howls hushed.

She sings into smoke and crackling wood,
But the voice that returns
Belongs to someone else,
A woman tied, slapped, and swollen.

She appeared four days ago,
Entering thatched and opened door,
Trembling, almost whispering,
Asking for three vials along the shelf.
Said she needed them for her man,
For the fists he burns into her breasts,
For the words that always leave her
Blue-black and alone.
Long Woman rocks back and forth,
Closes her eyes and sees
The visitor now pleading for her hand.
Can you help me, he asks,
Please, can you help me?

But what she knows makes her rise.
And what she softly chants
With bowed head and clasped hands,
Makes him still.

So still the moon quiets the owl.
So still no flame remains
Beneath the firefly's starless wings.

Rooted and Broken

My bones are as stiff as the severed
Necks of fowl that hang behind both ears,
Their beaks angled towards dirt and stone,
So close I can hear the beat of slow blood
Metronoming into dry world,
So close I want to drink

What my hands have gathered
From this low-country priestess
Who walks with a slight left limp, barefoot
Leaving earth smooth and unbalanced.

She has spoken
In the tongue of ancient deities
As sandalwood burned and myth chanted
Over a carved wooden bowl
Now steadied between my fingers.

To this altar, this temple of thatched reprieve
I have come for removal,
For the splendor of gods,
The requisite dose
Of powdered liquid heart.

Take, and drink, Long Woman says

And into the bowl I stare
With eyes yellowed, the gaze
Of a man who has been rooted
By some strange mix of voices,
Secular concoctions of greed and tarot hair.

Take, and drink, Long Woman says

And into the bowl my tongue laps
Like skeletal kittens
The steaming burgundy fluid.

From the hills, a cock crows thrice.
Five serpents coil around aching ankles,
And my head jerks back,
As if waiting
For evening's cold embrace,
The first drops of rain in my mouth,
Like forgiveness, unrequited
And broken into fits of shaking screams.

Drum Dream Dance

Anklets in the cowried dust.
Dip
    Beat
Reverse.
Half-turn swirls
Moon and earth.

Carolinians
Haitians
Africans
Drums

      Scream that stolen scream.

Hands slap
Stop
Pound drummed skin.

Down from the hills,
In from the sweaty humid coast
So many voices float
Pained human pain.

Five snakes whip-quick tongue lash air.

The center rises, the circle rattles

Half-turn swirls
Moon and earth.

Dip
    Beat
Reverse.

Scream that stolen scream.

Torch-fire smokes and flickers,
A child runs twice around the flames.
In her hands
A thousand midnight whispers.

Long Woman flails
The circle cries in tongues.

Come come come

Turn stop jump.

This dance of fire knows

     Calls you by your name.

Back into the circle,
Long Woman chants and quakes,
Hailing souls ancient
Bursting from her skin.

Five snakes rise and hiss.
Her circle moans
In the cowried dust

Where evening beds a child

     And child sleeps and dreams

     With drum.

III :: *Blood Trade*

Black horses drive a mower through the weeds,
And there, a field rat, startled, squealing bleeds
His belly close to the ground. I see the blade,
Blood-stained, continue cutting weeds and shade.

—Jean Toomer

Regions

We have reached this region
With the aid of clocks
Circling the hours of six and eight.
At seven, we remembered
Once making love
With the same sense of rhythm
Attached to the stigma, time and place.

We have fallen ever since

For all things remote: never embracing
Voices that knock and plead
To be answered on arrival.
We do not hear
Our mothers and fathers

Not breathing in bedrooms. Their ears
Taking in calls for life
To be completed, strung up after dark
With the snap of a finger, a rope, a flame.
We do not hear

The winds of braided leather
Slicing sweat and flesh. The screams
Have now been grounded like ankles
Shipped in rows. Here

In this unsettled region,
We have landed. Unsure
If the sounds we do not gather
Ring out from stolen drums,

Or travel inside echoes, broken:
No longer there, but not quite here.

Southern Blood Trade

The one thing that never moved
Followed him again. Always there
Like grafted skin that would not take,
Rejected by the body it had been given.

On warm days there would be wasps
Invisible on a full new nest, attacking
When he tried to wipe away the blood
He had heard so little about,
As if silence would make it disappear,
Become phantom stigmata in a phantom dream.

At age seven, he knew blood
Didn't work that way.
He had once seen a cow
Mooless and stiff
On his grandparents' farm
Hanging from hind hooves
With a fresh slit in its throat.

Either blood gushes, drips, or flows.
That much he knew.

He reached out
And gathered its thick heavy wine
In his hands,
Placed it to his nose,
Then tongued the surface to his lips.

That taste, wet and raw, remained with him.

He wondered again years later
About blood, the degree or two he now knew
That was passed in anger
In the evening
Of some Southern unspeakable trade.

But he wanted it to speak,
To tell him where it came from
And why it traveled, uninvited
From one vein into so many others.

Veiled mouths had made it mythic,
Even larger than storied thieves
At the gates
Of old Negro graveyards.

When he thinks now about the taste
Still escaping from his mouth
He sees the cow,
Surrounded by a black-gray mist:
Horseflies and gnats
Staring back at him
As if to say, *give me what you have taken.*

Then he sees himself
Alone, swaying against summer's breeze
And someone else
In his bloodline dying
With the one drop of silence
That should belong to him.

Carolina Spring

The man in Ellison's novel
   Never spoke his name,
      Always a wounded silence.

It could have been Jesus
   In my dreams with him
      Saying I would one day have to murder

Voices, ones which flower each spring
   Like dogwoods behind my parents' home.
      As a boy I searched for signs

Grandma planted in me
   Of the cross on their blossoms:
      Four reddish indentations at the tips

Signifying blood; the thin brown branches
   Standing in for death,
      The death of limbs once larger

Ages ago, before Friday morning.
   I would rise
      With my back against the trunk

And imagine nails hammering
   Palms and feet. I knew the birds,
      Circling, were plotting my flesh,

The distant bark of a wild dog
   Fresh on my scent.
      The mind always closing in

On itself, as if a prayer
    Plant at evening, folding back to an image
        That deceived. So when they would come for me

With steel-clawed breath
    They would find me
        No longer there, speaking

In clamorous tongues, my body
    Still anchored to the dogwood,
        Far too invisible for voices,

Or was I
    Too far gone to hear,
        Too far gone to be heard?

September's Fire

A stranger suddenly strikes a match
And you watch as it flames
Towards his Marlboro 100
Like a close-up, slow-motion shot
Filmed in a city not quite whole.

Again, your thoughts collapse
Once, twice into the rubble of your bowels
As he flicks away smoke, ash, and butt.

The double-twist of his right boot heel
Leaves black-gray marks on the sidewalk
And you stare at the cigarette's crumpled body,
The singed tip of its head, the stillness of its chest
While small cracks in the pavement
Lead to veins of a dislodged arm,
One finger tapping Morse code—
A plea you cannot decipher.
The other fingers say nothing at all.

When you look up
The stranger's no longer there.
Has it been hours, days, months?

Walking home, you sense the city's distant calm,
Burnt tobacco clouding your head.
Or is it the smell of hair, skin, bone
Now trapped beneath your nostrils,
Bundled inside your nerves
As if tangled in an everlasting flame?

Children Along the Shore

What seems to fall from mouths of angels,
Wingless in the nascent light of dawn,

Can land on your tongue and fill your head
With a thousand fragrant oceans,
Reminding you of mother's arms
Even when earth appears asunder,
When countless seagulls have fallen
Sideways to the feet of shored children—
One wing visible, the other submerged,
Like distance between truth, reconciliation.

One after the other, they arrive
Until all we see is an ocean of birds,
A jihad of birds,
A tribunal of birds,
A bombing of birds.

Nothing now grows along the shore.
And when angels ascend,
Wingless above the fresh embers of dusk,
Will we gather what has fallen from their mouths,
Spilling from their voices?
Will we taste what remains of their bread,
Or will we, like machetes of flesh and stone,
Divide the world between us,
Filling cavernous arms with hollow wings?

Bonfires

When I reached the beach
They were already circling
The 2 a.m. bonfire.
Guitars strumming
Smoke entering, exiting bodies
Someone singing Bob Marley
Outkast, Grateful Dead
While in a distant world
The voice of God
Was beating drums
Into the skull of a singular voice
Round and round they danced
18, 20, 22 years old
Chanting songs into oblivion
As if this dream would never end
Then Johnny, with no shoes or shirt,
Leaps into the flames
All the while screaming
Into the half-full Maryland moon
Get down, get down, get down
he has a grenade
And the whole scene erupts
A roadside explosive here
An RPG there
Suicide bombers coming from the rear
Smoke giving color to the unknown
Revealing the places we now abhor:
Mosul, Ramadi, Falluja,
Kuwait, Samarra, Baghdad
And each night breeds
Successive raids
Successive bodies offered
To the flames
Of his one and empty God.

South by Southwest

Sometimes when you leave, you leave
My soul sprawled out on the back seat
Beside you naked, thinking: *There's something*
About the south, even in the west.

Today you came equipped: the whips
To beat me back
In time onto the streets, dogs
To eat my flesh, hoses
To drive me off
My feet against a wall
Crashing through a window. My god
How far we've come
Over
Or so the chorus goes,
One day we shall.

And on that dirt road
Huddled, we felt
Noises against the evening
Against the car
Would leave shadows
Would leave us
Never alone.

The Stranger

My dog Casey likes it here
Where water becomes shore
Where a dark eastern line
Yields to an arc of orange-red fire.
She stares into that light and barks
June through August
Until the world listens, brightens.

Today, we're early or the sun is not on time
So we stand and wait
As mallards splash or ascend.
Again, my thoughts return to Camus,
How Meursault, with gun in jacket, came across an Arab
On the beach in *The Stranger*,
How he fired five times
Before the Arab had a chance to stand,
How the Arab was always just The Arab,
Nameless, dead.
Casey's bark
Brings me back, raises the sun.
As always, I tell her, "It's a new and better day."
And she barks in agreement.

In an hour these waters will become blue.
A jogger or smoker will arrive. A fisherman will appear
On the boulders and think about anything other than fishing.
But for now, we're alone
And with my eyes still on the newness of the sun,
I give Casey's leash a gentle tug
As if to say, let's move on, but she doesn't respond.
I tug again, and again, the weight at the other end
Does not give. When I look down,
Casey is a man on his side,
Naked, handcuffed, covering his genitals, and pleading for mercy
In a foreign tongue:
"No, no, no" he shouts, as the collar sinks into his skin.

No passersby, no witnesses, no cameras.
Just a human on a leash
With the waters of the Chesapeake
Crashing against his ankles.

I know what Meursault would do,
And I know what some Americans would do,
But I'm no Meursault
And this morning I'm not sure how American I am
So I kneel, remove the collar, and hold him in my arms
Wondering the whole time
Why and how it had to come to this.

Back Home

We would yield for railway signs
Where roads converged
Like Confederate stars
Licensed between headlights
Or at times whiplashing the air
From Gaffney to the Low Country
In a stranger's front yard.

I was a teen when I noticed
Who lived in those houses
And steered those cars
Impaled with memories
Savage enough to help drive
Generations from home.

Red, white, and blue crosses
Screaming from jackets, shirts, caps:
"The South will rise again,"
"It's a Southern thing,
Y'all wouldn't understand."

I thought maybe their ancestors had fought
At Fort Sumter, or perhaps in Columbia
When it burned
From Federal fire to the ground.

I would wonder about heritage,
Slogans, gestures
That needed to stalk, year after year.

But now, when I pass through
These streets my parents call home,
Streets I once cruised,
I see them and feel
It's just good ol' Southern redneck pain
That fetters the mind,
Restricting the tongue
From transmitting the syllables,
Yes, it's true, we lost—
Yes, it's true,
The War is over.

The Forest

What you kill in yourself, you kill in others—
or maybe, just the other way around.
—David St. John

You know the forest:
Every morning the same stroll,
The same air licking your nose,
The same twigs breaking
Your thoughts into grass
Beneath clouds playing
A game of eclipse with the sun.

When it loses, you're the one
Alone in the passing.

Yesterday you saw a face
Choked to the neck
Of a branch ahead in the path. Both dangled
As if the sky held
Some means of comfort. Then broke
Across the red and golden
Floor of October.

You ran, scattering from the trail,
But it found you years later
Not noticing birds in full flight
Or insects swarming and hungry.

Only voices appeared: *Who's behind those trees—*
The ones on the other end
Of an otherwise empty forest?

Or what is it that grows
Beyond the rising part of earth

Forever sinking into your skin?

The Man in the Middle

When full moon glares down on me
With the weight of wasted years
She shows me what I am—
A jumbled heap of bones
Strewn at the feet of her throne
A man lost in the ashes of hot coals
Afraid of what can no longer be
Resurrected or even raised
Black-blindfolded to a scaffold that sways,
Wrists roped and knotted
A trap door wide as my shoulders
Beneath my feet
If it gives, I'm drowning in someone else's hell
If it holds, five men with rifles will fire
On the count of three
I know which one isn't firing blanks
It's always the one in the middle
That's what my good friend John once said,
"Coleman, it's always, always the man in the middle."
And I believe him. That's how I got here today,
By believing my good friend John
When he said, "Coleman,
if you're gonna walk
On thin ice, you might as well dance, my man."
So one night when I could no longer see
Bodies swaying before me
I danced and danced and danced
Until cracks appeared and widened.
Go ahead, do me a favor, drop the door,
Unload your rounds.

IV :: *Incantations*

I can call spirits from the vasty deep.
Why, so can I, or so can any man;
But will they come when you do call for them?

—*Shakespeare*

Dawn Desert Journey

I went there seeking communion
With the lost tribe of thinkers
Who wandered into a storm
Of dust and angry locusts,
Losing the tongues that had carried them
To a chorus of blindness
And silence.

I wanted to peel back
What remained of their glorious voices,
To fill my mouth with gods' spoken wisdom.

When I reached that place
Of dawn desert sand
I found them not quite preserved,
Hearing only my own feeble fingers
Caressing what I had wanted to be
Sacred, full of all good and perfect gifts.

I knelt there for hours,
Head bowed, sun rising against my neck,
And prayed for the simplest of things:
A drink of oasis,
The return of lonely creatures,
And one night and one night only
To hear, to feel, to know
What it means to be.

Words, Sweet and Absolute

I thought they would come to me
Perhaps inside a swift, constant whisper.
At least it was hoped
A dream would land
Onto page, and there
They would lead
Through all that is sweet and absolute.

Everywhere, there were wings,
As a Brubeck tune danced
In ⁹/₈ time. Still,
No brown feathers fell,

And again, I was left
To stand alone
Beneath the smooth, curved spine
Of air: brilliant are the breezes,
But on this day, they too chose silence.

What is one to do
When voices anxiously awaited
Do not glide into one's palm?

I asked this of a stranger once
While we sat in an airport
Watching countless planes take flight.
She whispered, "They will return.
Everything alive and moving will return."

Yes, I thought,
Later recalling the transitory
Nature of faith:
How it sometimes appears
Sacred, not quite grounded
In this, our other
And often lonely world.

Onslaught in the Upper Western Hemisphere

If this is not so, who can prove me false
And reduce my words to nothing?
—Job 24:25

Yesterday, a strong gust of wind
Blew through a rack of swollen cattle
Inside the butcher's shop
And carried downstream
An entire school of fish
Upside down, near the surface of the lake.

Today, air was finding its way home
When the first tender drops of rain fell.
Earth, again, mistook everything for blood
And moon was not allowed to appear.
Instead, a surrogate life
Carried us through the remaining hours.

Please, do not believe it all flashes before your eyes:
"Hey, it happened just like this in a dream once,
While father's ghost floated close to the ceiling."
No, that's not the way it happens at all.
It is more like finding one's self

Alone, midway through a sentence

Knowing once a period evolves,
That will mean the end
Of thought as we presently know it.
Yes—corridors, and an intricate sense or two—

That's the way it happens,
As if a glint of sun, bouncing
Off a butcher's shiny new blade.

60

The Man Who Thought Himself a Mother

There must be stars, Alex demanded,
Lots and lots of stars must exist,
And make sure the poem ends
With the word *death*, he said.

So stars were created.
Stars the size of a newborn's foot.
Stars small enough to fit in a newborn's hand.
There were scattered stars, abandoned stars,
Stars as random as a sleepless man's thoughts.

It was the fear of drifting into nothingness
That kept Alex awake all night,
Fear of entering night-world,
Fear of what he called the great abyss behind each eyelid.
No real man, no great man ever slept much, he said.
And more than anything, Alex wanted to be a real man,
A great man, the kind of man who did things no other man could.

Sleepless and delirious, he always spoke of stars, planets, galaxies.
He spoke of spiral galaxies, elliptical galaxies, irregular galaxies.
He even thought himself a comet once
On a collision course with an asteroid
The kind dinosaurs couldn't outrun.
He thought himself post-Triassic, pre-Jurassic,
But he never thought himself a dinosaur
Or a meat-eating reptile of any kind.
No, he had always been human, all too human,
But for now, on this day, he was a comet.

Alex, as a comet, crashed, of course
And when he awakened,
Four masked humans in matching green gowns
Had carved open his chest

And were wiping the bodies of two birds found inside.
They were covered in black, the birds,
As if washed ashore by an oil spill.
The masked humans slapped them
Until they let out a birdcry.
They were held up to the light,
Weighed, measured for length
And placed in folded blankets
Like two small-beaked burritos.

Euphoric and disillusioned, Alex thought himself a mother
And assumed the birds his twins.
For the very first time in his life, Alex cried.
He cried a birdcry, a humancry, a cometcry.
He jumped out of bed, grabbed his twins
Then ran outside to look at the stars.

There, in the soft white light of ten billion trillion newborns
He thought himself more mythic than tragic,
More Daedalus than Icarus
So he made himself a pair of wings
From feathers, wax, and thread.
With his babies strapped to a single breast each,
He escaped to the stars, planets, galaxies,
Especially those strange, irregular galaxies.

It was like dying, he thought,
Like being reborn or born again, he said,
Which for Alex had always been the better half
Of almost any kind of death.

Flight of the Blue Heron

5:30 a.m. and I'm alone
With birds I do not know
Yet they serenade me
In five different languages.

I've never stood beneath your window
To offer my raised and broken voice
But I have sat on this winding beach
For a year of mornings
Hoping you would hear my songs—
Waves, wind, words.

Across calm silk folds of sky-water
A blue heron has just taken flight
Gently flapping eastward
Gliding as if she knows the sun
Has just risen orange
Behind low gray clouds
As if she knows her way
Beyond the bridge near your home.

When you see her from your balcony
Please greet her
In a language you do not understand.
She will flap twice
Then open up and sing for you
All the music we have ever shared
All the soft rhythms soon to arrive.

Zero Sum Cathedral

Scientists have discovered wounds,
Peeled across the floor of the cathedral
Just miles from where you were born.
They say it is a theoretical advance
(not quite a miracle)
Clearly reflecting the way Christ
Once smothered skin with burning sand
During a bout of pre-dawn contemplation.

At least this is what we were told
The evening moon placed stone to lips—

Here, off the coast of the Atlantic,
Where we first heard your parents
Praying, as if to ward off a storm.

But what do they know?
I mean, scientists.
I am sure meteors sometimes shower
Undetected, during a blink of telescopes' brow.
It reminds me of an afternoon
We made love by mistake
With the curtains fully open:

Neighbors passed our window,
But no one seemed to notice
The way hair along the back of arms
Became erect every time
Your eyes appeared,
Then withdrew.

Afterwards, we visited the cathedral
With slices of serrated glass—

Scraped them back and forth along our legs
And spoke of Christ
Of the way millions worship daily,
Like that evening,
When a wave suddenly slapped
Your father below his unclothed waist
Causing him to stammer, in mid-prayer, then shout
Goddamn it!—Goddamn it!—Goddamn it!

Though he did not mean it.

Body Art Theatre

Torture is what it was like,
The way birds plucked hairs from flesh.
Was he now a Hitchcock woman
In cut-away black and white frames;
Or wounded raccoon, possum, deer,
Anything vulnerable
From an afternoon sky
Darkened with wings hovering?

For three days he and his wife sat handcuffed,
Operas of transcendence in their heads.
Others were shot or carved with razors
Until dragons blossomed
Across the crevices of their breasts.

One woman sought divine levitation
From a bed laced with rose thorns.
Red, yellow, and white petals strewn beneath the stems.

Viewers wanted to pray for her,
Make her rise from the garden.

Everyone wanted to gather
The beauty of it all, her blood
Like incensed oils blessed
Dripping above the curve of her spine.

When she finally rose, horizontal
As a leaf floating on water,
Sparrows sprouted
From each limb, swinging her away—
Grainy gray frames dissolved,
Black as full moon repose.

The crowd stood, unable to move
Staring into near absence,
Amazed by a sudden shaft of light
Now resting where their eyes had been.

Gratitude

Across the shore stands a tree
I shoveled to the ground
When I was eleven
While my father and uncle watched,
Telling me how my mother
Had wanted them to plant a maple
When I was born. "Yeah, right,"
My father told her, "Let him plant it himself."
So I did, listening to the men chatter
About the virtues of hand-to-earth labor,
About the importance of doing things
For one's self, about valuing sweat,
Calluses, tired muscles.

Now I'm seventy-five and sailing alone
Up the Chesapeake
Amazed by the power
Of my family's old binoculars,
Remembering the day I stomped
The last pile of dirt around the tree.
"Good job, young man," my father and uncle said,
"Good job indeed." I smiled,
Not letting on that I wanted to drop
My weary body down
To the base of the small tree and sleep forever.

In high school I would sit there and write
Poems to the river, to lovers
Both real and imagined. There were haikus
About leaves and grass, couplets
About unrequited longings.
My friends thought I was strange,
Wondered why I wrote and talked to myself.
But in the end they would always nod
And say, "Good job, young man. Good job indeed."

Yes, it's a beautiful sight: my tall adult maple
And the young couple beneath it
Valuing the shade of an old tree—
Unclothed, their bodies moving slower than the waves
That keep me afloat
But faster than the pulsing muscle
Housed beneath my flesh and ribs.

Are they in love, I wonder.
Does he stuff lines and verses
Through the vents of her high school locker?
Does she dream him at night?
Will he ever call again?

I want to and know that I should
Turn away, avert my eyes, drop the binoculars,
But how can I?
After all these years, it still feels good
To know someone appreciates my work.

After the Initial Slap: Ars Poetica

I

Life seems to flow
With unexpected motions
Of those caught in a world
Not fully imagined or literal.
Somewhere else, then
Is where our days must lead us,
With the two former options remaining
Options. "Come!"
Voices from outside the room shouted.

II

When I arrived, I heard:

Speak, damn it!
We want to know what happened
After the initial slap
For we have all been slapped
Ever since: the gods, oracles, magicians
We harbor. There had to be origins.
This is the geometry we are after.

III

Speak, damn it! The way we have
On nights when all else seemed
Buried beneath our breath,
Missing. We mean, knowledge
Of why we have been drawn
To this ragged stage
To perform feats, immortal:
At times, saviors who never wince—
Or else, we sulk here, rejoicing
In whispers under oceans,
Calling answers
Contemplation, form.

IV

And the silence?
What to make of it
When our beckoning fails?
When dismembered bystanders,
Forgotten in the meditation of nothing,
Appear murdered, unremembered

V

Here, on the periphery of thought
Where nothing has ever been fought and won,
Yet we often allow to sift between us
An instinct or intangible biology
That confines us.

Or, as Plato once claimed,
"Sight and hearing are powers,
If you really understand what sort of things I mean."
We mean, let's trudge ahead
Even at the sight of dusty coffles
Now entering the room,
Bringing with them the stale breath of panic
That this will be the day
Someone or something finally does us in:
A former minion, a cup of coffee.
A sharp word to the jugular.
A word that slaps and, in turn,
Blinds, deafens, enslaves.

Another voice said:

Let's move on

VI

To sunlight whistling through blinds every morning.
To nothing as sacred

As the last words
Left swimming in air from her breath.

And I know of no other
State in which my real self

Feels the need to join another.
Both halves are no longer halves.

On these evenings, I've heard the mutterings
Of quietly nestled stars between us.

VII

Another voice replied:

But the truth is,
Actors can change
Costumes and names
As easily as the word
Hello can become hello.
And then they're gone—
Portions of our selves float out the door
On the hems of skirts or trousers
Never fully to return.

It's a tricky trade: Trust.
But I trust the page, the wind,
The greatness of it
And all the qualities of creatures
Able to remain afloat.

VIII

Two, three, four clouds I see, and
If the page is a broken sky, then the pen,
Well, it has to be a bird, a plane, no
A ship at the mercy of a not-yet-seen Hero,

Transporting passengers before us, like images
Fleshed out and fragile in deep sleep
Where we all gather
Never to hear again
Language which sails above, across
Films of receding oceans.

Here, we are alone
With buildings and the stench
Of those once breathing.
The streets
Call out for fresh voices.
But the page, the wind,
Responds with nights of broken glass,
And the glass we walk upon naked,
With the shards
We circumcise our screams.

Again, we're unclothed and touching
Only the air between us.
This is the geometry we are after.
We have all been slapped.
There had to be origins.

IX

In unison, they shouted:

Speak, damn it! Speak!

V :: *Hunger's Embrace*

Occasionally, however, the rustle of a skirt hushes when they wake, and the knuckles brushing a cheek in sleep seem to belong to the sleeper. Sometimes the photograph of a close friend or relative—looked at too long—shifts, and something more familiar than the dear face itself moves there. They can touch it if they like, but don't, because they know things will never be the same if they do.

—Toni Morrison

The Color of Nepal's Flag

The final shadow may close my eyes,
carry me off from white of day,
unchaining my soul at the hour
of its anxious obsequious desire
                    —Francisco de Quevedo

An osprey swoops and gathers breakfast
Squawking *good morning good morning good morning*
As he lifts into a sun that bobs across waves
One leapfrogging the other
In a frenzied game of king of the hill
Splashing off the backs of horseshoe crabs
Washed up and entrenched along shore's edge
Like a dark brown line of defense
Between this and some other world.

In a moonlit garden a crown prince is convulsing,
The amnesia of hashish and bourbon on his breath
His mouth a hollow painter's palette
With bubbles the color of Nepal's flag
Streaming down his chin
Spilling onto the palace's unsoiled grounds,
Its storied kinship, its opulent mythology.

Here in Kathmandu some say his father,
The king, was Vishnu incarnate
An avatar, a keeper of Brahma's promise.
Some say his mother, the queen,
Was a pillar between son and fiancée,
An outsider from a lower rung
Daughter of a rival clan.
Some say "It was an accidental firing
Of an automatic weapon.
Seven members of the royal family are dead."

In a moonlit garden the crown prince remembers
Nothing of the smell of gunpowder on his fingers
And the M-16 stretched across his lap
Is silent in its warmth, as if melting
Into the language of his battle fatigues.

Mother, father, sister, brother
All silent as the dust
That now flees Friday evening stars.
When he removes his right hand
From his left breast pocket
Devyani's folded face rises
From his palm, her eyes appearing to speak
In a hush he has carried for twelve years,
Since the night his thoughts first allowed
The word *princess* to swim through his veins,
To dance like wonder inside his blood.

What are you saying, he asks, *what are you saying*?

As the trigger collapses her voice bellows
Throughout the countryside
From the Tarai to the Himalayas and back again
Until thousands have gathered in the streets
Shouting for answers they do not want to hear.

When I look up, the fish is still impaled
Beneath the osprey's ribs,
Alive and sometimes flapping dazed,
Knowing if he breaks loose he will be home again.
If not, he has seen for the first and last time
What breathes beyond water's plane—
The sun drugging the three of us
While eight horseshoe crabs march towards me,
Their shells as hard as helmets of palace guards
Rushing to save what has already been lost,
Their shells as warm as lids of polished urns
Protecting the remains of a wooden funeral pyre.

Blues Sarcoma

Rumor says you no longer dance
Manhattan's darkness, or dream
Of scaling the Empire State Building

With one hand tied behind your back,
Eyes closed so as not to see
The lives you know so well

Dangling like battered marionettes.
They say you, too, now undress,
Shower and live in the dark

Out of fear of being seen and seeing
Another bruise along your thigh,
Lesion across your temple

Or a sunken glow to your skin.
They say you sit there
Wondering how many of us

Have surrendered with you
To a rhythm so inward, so driven,
Not even the uptown number 6

Can outpace its lone, low beat.
They say it sounds like a man
Howling. They say it sounds like a woman

Bound. They say it sounds like once-sweet music,
The kind bodies moan when the mind sings,
Baby, baby, baby, I already done left this town.

Symbiosis

I miss afternoon's breeze—
The way it sauntered into the room
All the silence of last night's words.
I miss the way one tree would lean towards another,
Once the breeze entered,
And whisper, "Shhh. Let's watch, our work is done."
I miss the way my eyes would fade and eyelids close,
Once the breeze entered,
Then land outside to glimpse the nimble dance
Between sun and shadow. It frightened me
The way one suddenly consumed the other,
How complicit each was in the other's desire,
How they both fed from the same swollen pond
While water lilies burst into bellies of ripe pink-whiteness.

Blue dragonfly. Darting tadpole. One-eyed goldfish.
Did they know how quickly they left one world for another
As afternoon's breeze nudged
Beds of roses closer together
Sending their red-yellow scent into the room
Slowly opening my eyes?
Someone stood and closed the windows once
But it was too late:
A couple of birds were already passing
Small, cumulus clouds,
Each with the other's voice
Inside the other's ear.
We said nothing, but the breeze felt wonderful.

Desire's Madness

Is it possible to love
The absence of what we know is there,
The high arcing flights
Of what we may think we want,
The sharp sudden cliffs
Of what we know we can never have?

I want sweet bay magnolias
Kissing my mother's name.

I want drops of frankincense,
Three on my lips in a pure white field.

I want soft rain
Returning grandmother's final memory.

I want the equivalence of touch
When my body leaves my body.

I want wings—
Yes, diaphanous, ubiquitous wings.

I want the goddess of things unknown
Unmasked beneath a springtime elm.

I want to confess inside her temple
Behind lush azaleas at noon.

I want the unrevised dreams
Of the ocean's evening muse.

I want pre-morning whitecaps
Chanting my father's ghost: *home, home, home.*

I want to wade into a world
Where desire always hangs
Swollen by nocturnal winds
Like an effigy set on fire
Twirling inside her maddening flames.

Separation

Sometimes it happens as quickly as this:
She drives, and from the passenger side

You arrive alone with words,
Hoping they will connect

In some romantic sense.
Think again: they have fallen

And that stream of ideas
You once thought infallible

Now blankets every streetlamp you pass.
On black slates of pavement, she stares

Driving as if the silence of two faces is too much
As if it cannot be reconciled

Or even tossed from the window
You have just opened to get a fresh breath.

Up goes the window.

And you turn to her wishing to say, "I'm sorry,"
But her eyes tell you words

Would now be useless, like the air
Vacuumed around you:

Nothing flowing any more
Until you land alone at your door

Without a sound, composed
As if a swarm of razors

Has suddenly feasted, floated
Off with the flesh of your tongue.

Alone in Presence of Air

I am speaking today of bridges
And swollen voices:

The way icicles constantly breed
In absence of words.

I am speaking of skeletons
We now consider broken bones,

Sockets of moons, canceled sunsets,
And the hungry stench of silence.

I am speaking of shafts
Separating sun from light:

Shapes of distance
Only flesh can consume.

I am speaking of evenings
Only memories now make love to.

I am speaking of air, fractured
And alone in presence of air.

Lately, I have grown away from bodies,
Bodies I once thought could be my own.

I have watched my selves disappear
Like phantoms sprawled and lost

In a room of ancient whispers.
And I am no longer sure

If syllables we once embraced
Are asking to be held,

Or thrown away and forgotten.
Today I can only speak,

And leave you nothing more than this:
Nothing more than a voice

We used to share—
A voice

Now swollen, frozen
In the absence of our words.

Rock Cold Bone of Breast

Beneath the words she will not speak,
A shadow forms voiceless shadows,
Trapped between tongue and time.

And air, pressed to her teeth
No longer entertains thoughts of sound.
This air, like the man

Now tiptoeing the railings of a bridge,
No longer debates escape.
Both know expressions before have led to this,

That a simple push or thrust at this moment
Would mean not-so-simple things, unlike before
When a push of the tongue, or a thrust of the waist

Meant woman and man could unite no further:
Both motions meant no air, no shadows
Could pass between them.

But now, whether she breathes or not, he will
Stare into the roar of stillness,
Balanced like gulls atop barriers,

And exhale a distant, evening scream
As he feels the wind wrap itself,
The way she once did, around him

Head-first through rock cold bone of breast,
A body that will no longer part,
Not even for the howls now echoing through her ribs.

Always Hearing

Tell me again about voices
That descended, saying, "We cannot go back."
I have forgotten what you said
About the shape of the world's geography
About the way it unfurls in desert browns
How the hues of mountains at sunset
Taste like half-ripened fruit on a lover's lips.

Tell me again about voices
That fell into your palms, saying, "We cannot stay here."
You said we should obey
As if children nestled between mystery
And memory. So we moved
To a place that smells like rain on geraniums.
Now, when the sun awakens, I swear it sounds like a cymbal
Clashing overhead with horns, something Gabriel would play
If not for the handful of sins we have tongued
And swallowed. No, we cannot stay here, you said
And we cannot go back, but I think at times you forget

How I cradled one evening the heart of a cactus,
Its bright yellow flower, and spoke into its womb
How I stretched out on my back with the stars
Kissing the petals, how the near-full moon
Passed slowly beneath Jupiter, so close I thought they would touch,
So close I thought they would dance the dance
Pre-lovers dance, then run off to some dark and quiet world.

Sometimes I think you forget
How I placed the blossom between my fingers
How there was only the ache of knowing
How there was only the sound of longing
How I am always hearing, receiving
But they are voices you know I can never survive.

In the Arms of Snow and Darkness

What did night dream before?

Was I flying again
Between the angel of understanding
And all things tangled and wounded,
The sky filled with absolution and fear

Or was I wondering again
If we would or wouldn't speak
Beneath a sun of windblown leaves
While honeymusic glides between our lips?

Do you remember the taste of evening
When the room filled with white feathers and silence,
When wings sprouted from voices down the hall,
When each door opened another door,
When each window battened down hush-hushes?

I recall the beating of wings,
The pummeling of air
Through each heart's separate chambers.
What we found is what was there.
What was there is all we have.

I recall the beating of wings,
The chasm between lives
When trees were left bare,
When my body floated in the distance
In a pine-box tomb
Set ablaze and shoved across the ocean
Wrapped in ancient white muslin
Burning in the middle of hunger
Burning in the absence of sound
Burning in the arms of snow and darkness
For thirty-three nights and a day
Until the beating of wings returned
And rushed me to the shore,
Ashened, awakened, anew.

Fragments of Sand Flying

The hour had not yet conceived breath: Silent
In the background of mountains, cactus.

Heat. Gliding closer to our skin, air
Licked, circled back and became nothing more

Than first light air. Contained by the balcony,
We surrendered our glances: mine left

The one silver streak of her hair
And settled for a blur of sunlight

Beneath the blue pigeon's wing. She moved,
And said somewhere there is an hourglass

Emptying: She saw fragments of sand flying
As if to be with someone, or to escape some thing.

She said, the air about the sand was kind, the kind that says
When one grain blows north and another west

Distance sometimes claws and leaves broken spaces,
At others, she said, it just claws,

And never leaves.

First Anniversary: Virginia Beach

What was there not to desire
Last evening by the pool

With wind flowers, crescent flesh
And the still-fragrant kiss

Of Liebert's "Thru the trees/Cloudless Sky"?
I wanted you then and I want you now

To know that inside the bodies we carry
Are a thousand swollen remnants,

Memories, and the lone breath
Of quilted light, coupling

Every line of thought, serenaded
By the squeak-squawk voices

Of seagulls in midflight,
Their language unknown yet understood

And once the Atlantic rises and waves
Every word the earth has ever spoken

Seems to crash upon sand,
Embracing our ankles

Refusing to let go.

Morning Quatrains

for Ynez

When daylight arrived, shrouded
In the pretext of morning
Fog, I had almost forgotten what it was
I wanted to say.

Then soft air landed
On the balcony
Of pink and fuchsia impatiens,
The ones that seduce hummingbirds

Like clockwork each noon
As the sun crawls onto wooden planks,
Serene under shadows
Of black metal railings

Where warmth dances against my skin
And I am kissing my wife
Who is miles away
Charting the delicate flow

Of misguided hands,
How automobiles clash
As if bumblebees tangling
Over a bright yellow sunflower.

I want to tell her I'm safe,
That I miss her
Here, amid words gently colliding
Among the countless seedlings

That have now grown like children.
When I water them, I say,
"She'll be home around six."
And they always listen,

Drinking what I whisper,
Thoughts of her
Sinking into their roots,
As I turn them, I hear them sing her name.

About the Author

Jeffrey Lamar Coleman grew up in Gaffney, S.C. and is an Associate Professor of English at St. Mary's College of Maryland. He received a B.A. in Communications from Winthrop University, an M.F.A. in Creative Writing from Arizona State University, and a Ph.D. in American Studies from the University of New Mexico. His poetry and essays have appeared in several publications, including *Brilliant Corners: A Journal of Jazz and Literature, Blue Mesa Review, Critical Essays on Alice Walker, Rattle: Poetry for the 21st Century, Black Bear Review,* and *The Journal of Social and Political Thought.* He lives in St. Leonard, Maryland, with his wife, Ynez, and two children, Nadia and Javier.